POEMS 3

POEMS

Alan Dugan

Yale University Press

New Haven and London

1967

Published with assistance from the
Mary Cady Tew Memorial Fund.

Acknowledgment is made to the following publications for poems
which originally appeared in them:

Jeopardy: "Night Song for a Boy"

New American Review: "Idyll of Ascension"

The New York Review of Books: "Expenses"

Poetry: "Flower Grower in Aquarius"; "Conspiracy of Two
against the World"; "The Working World's Bloody Flux"; "His
Hands Have Five Knives Each"; "On Being Out-Classed by
Class"; "Barefoot for a Scorpion"; Poem ("Oh that was not a
scrap of flying Daily News"); Poem ("Flowering balls"); "Variation on Themes by Roethke & Eliot"; "On Rape Unattempted";
"On Zero"

The Poetry Bag: Poem ("It is no wonder that new lovers run");
"Against Solitude," now retitled "American against Solitude";
"Nostalgia for a Language"; Poem ("On the old bridge, the
bridge"), retitled "Advertising in Paris"; "A Hope against Pollution"

Wascana Review: Poem ("The tree was wet with the moon's . . .");
"Brutalization under the Heart of Peace"; "Northern Statement
for St. Cecilia"

For Judy

CONTENTS

Flower Grower in Aquarius   1
On Being Out-Classed by Class   2
Against a Sickness: To the
Female Double Principle God   3
The Working World's Bloody Flux   5
Poem   6
Not to Choose   7
American against Solitude   9
One Waking in a Northern Fall   10
Memory of Old Forms under Hell's Angels   11
A Hope against Pollution   12
Qualifications of Survivors   13
Adultery   14
On Zero   15
Poem   19
Self-Exhortation on Military Themes   20
Let Heroes Account to Love   21
Two Hatreds of Action   22
For an Obligate Parasite   24
Elegy for a Puritan Conscience   25
Expenses   26
The Butcher!, Borges, What a Shock!   27
Poem   29
On Gaining a Soul   30
On a Snake   31
Barefoot for a Scorpion   32
Idyll of Ascension   33

On a Hymn, Misprinted   34
Brutalization under the Heart of Peace   35
Poem   36
Poem   37
Variation on Themes by Roethke and Eliot   38
On Alexander and Aristotle, on a
Black-on-Red Greek Plate   39
Night Song for a Boy   41
For Lisa   42
Advertising in Paris   43
On Work   44
Poem   45
Noon's World   46
Poem   47
The Attempted Rescue   48
On Rape Unattempted   49
Conspiracy of Two against the World   50
Nostalgia for a Language   51
There He Was   52
Narcissus II   53
Poem   54
Poem   55
His Hands Have Fives Knives Each   56
Sailing to Jerusalem   57
Northern Statement for St. Cecilia   58
A Trial   59
Jewels of Indoor Glass   60
"I Have Met the Enemy and I Am Theirs"   61

POEMS 3

I fell away toward death
for lack of company and goods:
no business but to flinch.
A woman caught me with the hook
her smile wore at its edge
and wound me up with a winch.
Love's bucket, I was refilled!
So I came back and kissed
and cursed her. She fixed lunch.
She gave me solid grounds,
the company of laughter,
and the water works. Oh I
recant! I should invest
in fly-by-night concerns
while I have flesh to risk
and currency to burn,
so I will hang around
her wellhead and decant
death's water to my drawer.

ON BEING OUT-CLASSED BY CLASS

You
say,
"You
can't
be
any
good
because
you
aren't
some
one
from
some
place."
Ha!

Where I came from is torn down,
where I'm at is condemned,
and where I'm going to
is not built up yet. My Grand
Father steamed away from yours
for eats! regards! and joys.
Better to be Dugan the Cop
and never talk about a shitty past
than to be classed out
of the potatoes in the old
sod. He dreamed America up, and I
played Indian against
his cowboy lies because:
tradition is for the rich
to love, the clerks
to ape, the poor
to suffer, so I wander
to take the air, regards, and joys.
Where are they? You
will tell me. Anyone
free of your slavery
is better off in his own,
so Up the five-hour day!
Up art! Up the I.R.A.!

AGAINST A SICKNESS: TO THE
FEMALE DOUBLE PRINCIPLE GOD

She said: "I'm god and all
of this and that world and love
garbage and slaughter all the time
and spring once a year. Once a year
I like to love. You can adjust
to the discipline or not,
and your sacrificial act
called 'Fruitfulness in Decay'
would be pleasing to me
as long as you did it with joy.
Otherwise, the prayer 'Decay,
Ripe in the Fruitfulness'
will do if you have to despair."

Prayer

You know that girl of yours
I liked? The one with strong legs,
grey eyes, weak in the chest
but always bouncing around?
The one they call "The Laugh,"
"The Walk," "That Cunt," "The Brain,"
"Talker, Talker, Talker," and
"The Iron Woman"? Well,
she's gone, gone gone, gone
gone gone to someone else,
and now they say that she,
"My Good," "My True," "My Beautiful,"

3

is sick to her god-damned
stomach and rejects all
medication. What do you do
to your physical praisers that
they fall apart so fast
or leave me? She needs help now,
yours or that prick's,
I don't know which.

    "I have worked out
    my best in belief
    of the rule, 'The best
    for the best results
    in love of the best,'
    or, 'To hell with it:
    I am just god:
    it's not my problem.' "

I will sit out this passion
unreconciled, thanks: there are
too many voices. My visions
are not causal but final:
there's no place to go to
but on. I'll dance at the ends
of the white strings of nerves
and love for a while, your slave.
Oh stupid condition, I drink
to your Presences in hope of sleep
asleep, and continuity awake.

What do you do if you meet a witch?
Move! from the scenery of belief in her
by air, by car, by foot, by back-
roads if you must, but move! Leave!
And if you can't or think you can't,
Oh build a fort of reason in her country,
and walk the battlements of stone,
of brick, of mud, of sticks, of thorn-
bush if you lack, and say the charm:
"2 plus 2 is four," a truth so true
it laughs: "Tautology! Tautology!" before
the numbers change in speech and come
in screams, in shouts, in lalling, or
in curses if you hurt. 2 plus 2
is Noah's Ark, with every couple in it
coupled into one and crying differently
to make a third, a fourth, a fifth, a litter.
Dove, find us a land of peace and ease.
Come back with a bomb or burning bough
proof in your claws that love or death,
in giving us the business, gives us all.

POEM

A man applying gold leaf
to the window's word backwards
combed his hair to charge
his gilder's tip with static,
so he charged his hair with gold.
He was electrically the gold-
haired father of the gold word
GOODS! and god of the store's
attractions. When he waved his maul-
stick I went in to buy
the body of his mystery.

I should be someplace else!,
but pace around in the sweats
of inhumane endeavor and its trash:
goods, deeds, credits, debts.
Have it your own way, life:
I'm just here to die, but I
would rather live it out as a fool
and have a short life in contempt
and idle graces, but, instead,
the office telephone goes off
and voices out of its dark night
command me, "Choose, Choose,"
while women's angel voices call
the cities and their numbers. Then,
when I do choose: "I run away!"
the shop door opens and a cop
or statue stands there in the way.
What does he want? Blood. Oh
let me tumble in the wards, bolts,
and chambers of a police lock locked
so I can get to sleep again,
warm in the guaranteed steel!
Instead, I have to fake him off
with promises to pay. Cash!
How cold action is. I should
do spiritual exercises toward
the body of this world
and get in shape for choices,

choices, No! Instead, I leave
the dirty business by the back
window, climb down the fire escape,
and sneak off out of town alive
with petty cash and bad nerves in
an old Ford with a broken muffler!
So here I am again, July,
vacationing in your country broke,
in debt, not bankrupt yet!
and free to get your message!
What is it?
To begin again in another state!

Ah to be alone and uninhibited!
To make mistakes in private, then
to show a good thing! But that's
not possible: it's in the Close of life
that towering Virtù happens. Why
be absent from the wheeling world?
It is an education! Act by act,
Futures materialize! So, go deal,
old bones, enjoy it while you may!:
eat, drink, think, and love; oh even work!,
as if all horrors are mistakes,
and make the social product: new
invisible skies arriving! full
of life, death, insanity, and grace!

The red curtain moving in the still room
is frightening in portent to me housed.
The heart, in its choice cage of ribs, pounds
as if the air, which was a hurricane
all up the dangerous Atlantic coast
with gross waves and accumulative clouds,
has petered out into an indoor draught
telling the officed brain, high up inside
the dead air of its hairy capitol dome
but sensitive as a bat to every draught,
that revolutionary storms are happening down there!
to move the red curtain in the still room.

The old road followed
the lay of the land
to fords. It went
commercially to towns
around it, curving
in respect to rocks
and skirting pastures,
but the Imperial Road
denied the map relief
and spanned its rapids.
It crossed and climbed,
regardless of contour,
straight as a weapon
should be. Now,
with both disused,
and armed pilgrims
walking cross-country
to avoid the air's
condors and fliers, who
can say which road
travelled the better
to what end, or how
the travelling was
that got us nowhere,
under hell's angels.

There is smoke over the river at the end of the street.
Something is happening, because the air is full of news.
An arriver or departer is arriving or departing and
displaces tons of water up against the rotten piers.
The gutters run with it. I hope that she or it
will bring or take a cargo of the manifest goods
and not that plague that goes from there to here
or here to there in rats' nests in the bilge beneath
the blue and white flag of the Scandinavian sky.

Hide in cesspools, sleep well
on broken glass, and eat
shit. Kiss the whips,
hold the wife for rape,
and have good luck:
stumble behind a lamb
before the bomb bursts
and crawl out of the wreck
to be the epitaph:
"The good ones die first,
but I am not so bad:
Americans are worse."

ADULTERY

What do a few crimes
matter in a good life?
Adultery is not so bad.
You think yourself too old
for loving, gone in the guts
and charms, but a woman says,
"I love you," a drunken lie,
and down you go on the grass
outside the party. You rejoin
the wife, delighted and renewed!
She's grateful but goes out
with a bruiser. Blood
passions arise and die
in lawyers' smiles, a few
children suffer for life,
and that's all. But: One
memo from that McNamara and his band
can kill a city of lives
and the life of cities, too,
while L.B. "Killer" Johnson And His Napalm Boys
sit singing by their fire:
The Goldberg Variations.
So, what do a few crimes
matter in a neutral life?
They pray the insignificance
of most private behavior.

The man who first saw nothing
drew a line around it
shaped like a kiss or gasp
or any of the lips' expressions during shock,
and what had been interior
welled from its human source
and pooled, a mirror perilous.
That was the mouth of the horn of agony,
the womb all matter tumbled out of in the first
meaningless avalanche of the concrete,
and I'm afraid that it will be
the sewer of all water and the grave of space
so as to be complete.

When his head, dead tired of its theory,
dropped to the mark it made,
his forehead drank the kiss of nothing.
That was not sleep!
His students dove through it
down oceans of absence and
are not remembered, but
beautiful wet women ran out of the surf, subtly changed
and laughing over something secret they had learned.
Their navigating sons
sailed past horizons of the sensed
and founded wonderlands!
deep in the deserts of flesh away
from heaven's waters. They have not returned either.

I am not interested in mathematics
as a way of knowing, but
once I was the bravest acrobat
ever to leap through burning hoops!
Now I balk when I run at
my burning mirror, mouth, and twin,
afraid that I will not break out again
the other side of death,
applauded, unscorched, and agrin.
Oh I refuse that lovers' leap
through spit and image
down the throat of shock
and into the opposite day.
I am afraid that parity is lost
and nothing wins.

Once I calmed
myself before that chaos caught
so weakly in the charms of will
and called it cornucopia, cloaca, or else: nought;
but now the charmed
circle seems no longer to be charmed;
its wizards must have lost
the mumbo-jumbo that could call up
useful salamanders, fiends, and witches from the pit
and hold them helpless in the will
and tractable to Liberal errands.

Now when the fouls appear
howling and snorting fire,
who is to ride them out
fairly and full of honor like the knights
and to what businesses?
Whole governments of them
induce it at the world's heart,
all their citizens are food,
and it can drink the oceans,
eat the mountains, roots to peaks,
and bubble to the outer edge of air
to be a nova. "Istimirant Stella!"
strangers might say, and make their own
unearthly, efficient prophecies.

After sleepers first touch zero at the maw
they wake up in a permanently different light.
They wear its caste-mark as another eye
incapable of sleep or hurt, and burrowing inside.
They're fed to it; it
widens unastonished and they drown: internally.
If only I knew a woman's charm I cannot learn
in whose clear form and lines
the trouble of the problem slept, solved,
oh they would have a lid against its light,
rest in the mystery, and a chance
blindly to venture on in time,

but no such Cyclops
crazed by the price of size
would search the bellies of his sheep
to thank his blinders and their flame-sharp stick;
his eye is the condition of his flock
and his flock is his food and fleece;
so: sack the world's
unfinished business in your balls,
Ulysses, and escape
to soaking Venus or the red plains
of Mars: Nothing might be here.

18

What's the balm
for a dying life,
dope, drink, or Christ,
is there one?

I puke and choke
with it and find
no peace of mind
in flesh, and no hope.

It flows away
in mucous juice.
Nothing I can do
can make it stay,

so I give out
and water the garden: it
is all shit
for the flowers anyhow.

"Courage!" I say. Thus exhorting myself,
I say encouraging words the way the lame
Tyrtaeus was supposed to have been paid
to say them, making marching songs to make
whole Spartans march away in whole faith:

"Now hear this, you sons
of Hercules: God is on
our side, so make believe
black death is white as day.
Dress up your hair for war
as if for girls or boys
and throw your bodies away:
Love and your death are equal joys."

But in his own crippled song to himself,
"On Marching Lamely," he paid himself to say:

"Go it alone, kid.
Run your own races.
But when they say, 'Shit!'
squat and make faces."

All these men later died. His and their fame
goes on in all military routines,
while the counter-song I make him say
of army verse I've said and heard
goes on in enlisted men's latrines.

LET HEROES ACCOUNT TO LOVE

Statement	*Accounting*

I too was born out of a lion's mouth
and have the twenty-one longitudinal marks
of passage through the teeth to prove it:

Oh I am split up the middle half way,	1 slice
and once up either side, further up.	2 slices
These four strips got split up into fives each	8 slices
at their tips, since once the head was out	for the fingers
and chewed to features, then the teeth	8 slices
began to close, firmly: they clenched	for the toes
around the fingers and the toes. I pulled out!	
But where the main cut of the center teeth	
began, oh it is ragged and still hurts	2 slices
or wants or hopes, I don't know which,	for the penis
and strives to grow together in a whole.	(the
It's stiff in tantrum with this wish	balls
from time to time, since I was what was all	fell
there was inside the lionskin when I shucked it,	dual
and would come to you, love, past divides.	in
So when you see some hero's face	desire
framed in a lion's jaws and teeth,	later
do not be so impressed by valor's clothing.	on.)
Beast's puke, let him endure the tortures of undress.	—
Vomit your essence, Hercules. Be me:	21

1. Hero

If I were in the belly of the whale
I'd praise the peristalsis of my death
and play the bleeding cilia, I felt,
like clappers of my hopes' carillon! But
once I have been downed I find
the swimming hard in acid, hard among
the downed ferocities of sharks,
my swallowed brothers, so I war
with the living dead. Terror of peace
swallows the praise, because my parts
will go to feed the beast. Sharks and I,
once we have chewed identity to shreds,
will be Leviathan, the that which eats
the carnivores in combat through its bowels.
Sleep in its body and blood! That's all
the stomach joy there is among toothed souls.

2. Coward

I won a precious I
from selfless sleep. The bells,
whistles, and alarms of dawn
awoke me. Oh I was scared
and hung around in hell:
an Idyll. Then the flags
and brass band of the day
began to fly. The opted I
was drafted and fell in

behind the chest-boom of the drum
or public heart. I drummed within
and marched away, while my true love,
who gave the word to start,
ran weeping by my side.
Fifes drilled through my ears
and found my trouble: brains
coiled in the greys of self,
and reamed them with the shrieks
of civic cadence. Forward! I
was forced to march,
up to the point of fire! Halt!:
Did I win out of sleep
just to be worked and slain?
No! Oh I would rather sleep
well out of uniform,
be slapped and shouted at
by officers of the day,
and win my death at ease,
not in the army game!
but I say what the drum says:
boom. The fifes squeal WE.
My brains are drummed out
of the corpse and wheedled away.

Mother!, I am sick
of alcohol and grown up
foods. That blue milk
diet that I used to suck
is what I need. If you
give up your sour weeds
I will tear out
my permanently biting teeth
so we can be attached
again as sucker-shark
and shark, I mouthless on
you, and you savagely mouthed.
Oh we will course the Deeps
as pure efficiencies
where life obeys its first
imperative of desire: eat!,
and not the second: screw!
Oh I will close my eyes
so tight they disappear
in trusting sleep: who needs
them? Wills. Lovers. You.

ELEGY FOR A PURITAN CONSCIENCE

I closed my ears with stinging bugs
and sewed my eyelids shut
but heard a sucking at the dugs
and saw my parents rut.

I locked my jaw with rusty nails
and cured my tongue in lime
but ate and drank in garbage pails
and said these words of crime.

I crushed my scrotum with two stones
and drew my penis in
but felt your wound expect its own
and fell in love with sin.

I choked my frog on human crumbs.
My mother fainted when she saw
a toadstool growing from my thumb
and would not let me out of doors.
I drowned lead soldiers in the sink.
My parents fought a war downstairs.
My father lost me with a wink,
and grey pushed out his chocolate hair.
I found the toilet much too late
and stole away on roller skates,
hoping to find a cheaper law
behind the penny candy store.
I have the honor, love, to be
your animal, but will not please.

THE BUTCHER!, BORGES, WHAT A SHOCK!

—for Donald Mark Fall

*We have been well
and truly had.—Pascal*

What a jewel the view
is from the furnished room,
flashing with red, green,
and orange traffic lights:
That's dancing!, and it sings
as a general sound. What
a crystal air is,
metrical in structure,
clear in the open-work,
burning at its joints,
and moving in its bodies ordered everywhere
as force's products in pure chance.
What an honor to be in it,
even as a flaw, Oh
fracture of a tree in solid quartz!

Oh I had to look away
and down the open trap-
door in the center of the room,
into the cellar hole
where I have not yet fallen.
The man-faced bat-winged worm
looked up from his work
on my love's corpse falling,
his grin foul with his lights,
and said, "So what?, Faller,
I come in the works
of your love's wounds, foaming.
My sperm are his worms."

Love, I have known
you in your change
from spring to garbage, so
I ask you: Why
is the world so beautiful?

It has to be all sex
to make us want it here
against the worm's brief:
"I am the root and teeth.
What you dream I am.
You are the meat.
Fly if you can."

So: Beget sons against death.
Get real estates against decay,
and praise physical glory!:

The stars above the roof
are there as God's dust
at the center of this sphere
whose edge is nowhere.

—from *"Pascal's Sphere"*
by Jorge Luis Borges.

POEM

The Pythagorean Silences
opted for the flesh
and came and burned in it.
They thought, felt, and watched,
wanting some ecstasy.
Oh unaccountable spirits,
they take this on as choice,
get fated, and become,
out of their nothingness,
cropping summer of delight.
They like to burn in the sun.
There is, oh nervousness,
no granary at night:
the flying chaff of the stars
should demonstrate this thesis.
They like this life and death
and stare out of the stone
forehead of a horse
as if it were some sport.

ON GAINING A SOUL

As I explained the rules,
quarters, and conveniences,
the bloodless animal
I'll call "my soul"
tongued at my blackest tooth
in absent-minded joy
and asked about the truth
of feeling: it has a short
vacation in the flesh
and everything to do,
so I should take great pains
to satisfy the guest
so that it does not leave
before I make it pay.

ON A SNAKE

The snake on the blue
pool table of the moss
is denser than a stick
of equal girth and heavier,
for all its lightness and
slick ways, because its
muscles organized beneath
the overlapping platelets of
oiled parchment have to be
compact to make that tense
wobble of reaction that
you feel if you should pick
it up. Now that I know
the motto: DON'T TOUCH SNAKES,
and wear the diacritical marks
the two fangs make, I say,
"Man, you are smarter than it,
that muscular intelligence:
snap off its head!" The glass
snake, weighty and complex
in otherness, must think
the whole thought of the cold
when it is cold. He would
not know the drag end
of his tail from twigs
around him in the snow
when you are wiser warm,
dreaming of venom by the fire
where a cautery instrument
turns red, and healing rum
roars when the poker is dipped in.

The color of the sac and stinger of the scorpion
was red, and got its beauty from their poison. Bare
feet ache with the threat, the eyes with praise,
the serum for revulsion. Praise be, then, that
the armored teardrop searching on the tail
could miss feet, sting sight, and reconcile
death's stamping panic with a vision of form,
red at the point where chance and law join.

Clicking in rock pasturage,
the deer were delicate except
for grass sounds in their teeth
from nervous grazing.

Rightly addicted to shock,
fangless economies like these
mooing advocates of speed
posit a lion in ambush;

lying down with him
in ravin's daily dream,
they struggle out of flesh
under his padded paw.

"I am undone," sings the lion,
and leaps. His Worship
drinks at the throat's race,
swills in the hollow gut

spilling with sweets, sick
with private desire, and takes
the pasture-price for flesh:
his noble joy in rending.

So it all goes, upward
like the deer's pop eyes;
whoever devours the lion
tastes the deer's flavor.

Oh they were doing custom
slaughtering down Dead End Road.
Because I am a soldier of the Gross
I went to see
the soldier of the Lamb
get his. Such eyes!
such chops! such skin!
Oh shall I fear to own the cause
or blush to speak its name?
No! It's Murder! Murder!
I sail through bloody seas.

After the engagement they stacked their arms,
wrapped their hunger in the old stains
of lousy bandages, and fought themselves asleep
beneath a white-flowering tree.
Its bark was black with clear rain.
The red heart of peace, pecked at by a dove,
hung hidden by the flowers on a high branch
the way a ham is hung up from the dogs
to cure. Why hang a heart up
in the white disguises of a black-barked tree?
The birds will get it. Also: flowers fail: once
shaken harmonically by shots or shouts,
they fall together, or they shrivel in the stench
rising from the soldiers' dirty sleep
and fall to bare the red peace of heart.
Irregulars, arisen frightened in white rain,
go jump for it, grinning like dogs
because of want. They shoot it down
as an edible beast, or as a target, or
as something else to shoot. They make
their wounds gape and utter fearful cries.
They make the bird fly off for other forage.

The tree was wet with the moon's
red water when two souls
came down from flight outside the air.

They cried at the fall to flesh
among the snapping dogs on land
and the crawfish in the water

by the tree. Their cries condensed and held
as one dove on and one heart hung
from two different branches. The white dove sang

its love of hearts; the heart
wept blood at its danger. The night
turned blue to be the moon's lungs,
and the red tree its bronchia.

Oh that was not a scrap of flying Daily News
falling on the wind
that some kid caught
and held up laughing from a snapping dog:
That was the dove itself come down
to be the pigeon for the day
when captured love grows up
to any life it has in goods and children.

The child signed the steamed pane
with his nose and fingerprints. He drew
a heart's shape, the initials
of a beautiful stranger, and his own,
pierced by an arrow that was clear and cold.
The power of his waiting changed
to light: the lights came on
inside and out, it was so strong,
and then the smell of women, food,
and househeld pee was changed. Cloth
came in with short whiskers soaked
in beer, tobacco-smoke and air-
smells from the business of outside.
Strength moved through the rooms
laughing too loud and hard
for the long bead curtains of rules
around explosive plates and cracking chairs.
First as a marsupial of pockets, then
as a freehold bird swung in the air,
his knowledge of the world of god
expanded in a space too small for joy.

ON ALEXANDER AND ARISTOTLE, ON A
BLACK-ON-RED GREEK PLATE

The linear, encircled youth
acclaimed his limits running
in the bottom of a plate
with "he's a handsome lad"
scratched anyhow around
him as a joke or hint
of love. A northern prince,
finishing his cereal beneath
a Grecian tutor's smile,
would see the one clear line
appear, become a youth,
and run off on the way
from breakfast to the city
through an alphabet
circumferenced by art.
This is doubt's breakfast
in a school of Gordian knots:
in ending at the genitals,
where it began, the line
is doubled on itself and tied
unclearly in a bow knot
with dangles. The lewd
scratches mar design well.
Which way can princes turn
with The Philosopher behind
them and the Greeks in front?

If cooks can shatter art
then love is menial, and boys
can use it to be gods
in thirty-some-odd years.
That was doubt's breakfast
in the school of Gordian tricks:
"To have good government
thinkers should form the king,"
so when he took his way
he took Real armies with him:
Athens crumbled in the Seen
of Alexander's sober frown
and tricked his looking to go on
to Porus and the elephants
and drunkenness in Babylon.

Lock up the church,
I feel as unasleep
as a dead cat: regards
are what I want,
regards, regards, regards.
A priest after boy's ass
feels better than I
do: When I walk around
ladies on the stoops
think I am death: If I
had steel plates on my heels
Oh they would know it.
I should rape a saint
and she could save me
from the dangers of life.

May flowers of dirt and
flowers of rocketry both
be in your bunch, love,
when you get married out
beyond my death to you
and the world's wars.
Agreed! Oh she agrees
to anything for laughs,
love, and being danced
to records playing dances.

ADVERTISING IN PARIS

On the old bridge, the bridge
they call "New Bridge,"
a model wearing the brassiere
named "Triumph!" posed
on the archaic stone.
Novelty and persistence meet
in formal beauty
and what wins? The river.

ON WORK

The smell in the diamond morning was
of a restaurant cleaning up. Two men
carried a container full of slops
to a commercial garbage truck
and drove the night-time tares away
once appetite had made the day.

Portage of day from night to night,
I had hoped to sit in the staring sun
at bitter ease, cool in the tares
of will, and also wonder how to be
not part of it, the cartage, slops,
and increments of day. Who is to eat

with such an attitude?, wooing the world
with claims. Porters and their freights
form in the aches, so I must carry three
pieces of paper and a ball-point pen
from one desk to another for profit
while there is profit under the sun.

POEM

Always prudent but unprepared
for spontaneity in weather,
the office workers got their pressed
survival jackets soaked
while running in new rain
from work to travel home.
Some of the typists laughed
to feel real water not
from taps: they are the ones
with joys to dream of, once
the day is typed away. Once
I'd hoped to dream in the rain
for life, unbothered by
the economics of appearance,
and I did, for years, and knew
its soaking intimacy. Now
I'm pressed in the synthetics too,
and have no place to go
to in the weather, except home,
but it is not so bad,
pacing an empty office after 5
in the trash of squalid crises.
I hit the key of "I"
on a girl's machine, and see
that it is red, nail polish red,
with her device of getting on
beautifully for survival:
that is not just vanity!
I get rebellious for the truth
of outside weather often, but
my check is here each Friday.

The day is full of people, Sun,
walking around the staring noon
of paid endeavor: it is a shock
to someone who has slept apart
all morning in a shaded room
to come out into traffic. I
am hopelessly in arrears. I try
to catch up on the action, eat
a lunch for breakfast and pretend:
What have I missed except life?

POEM

A man with a box walked up to a woman with a boy, gave the box
to the boy, said, "Don't drop it for a change," and kissed
the woman, sucking up her rosebud from her mud-color. It bloomed.
He said, "Let's go." They went, with technicolor haloes of the usual
around them. Why? Because: They come from a star, live by its light,
and burn with it here in the dark outside of the department store.

THE ATTEMPTED RESCUE

I came out on the wrong
side of time and saw
the rescue party leave.
"How long must we wait?"
I said. "Forever. You
are too far gone to save,
too dangerous to carry off
the precipice, and frozen stiff
besides. So long. You
can have our brandy. That's life."

"Be alive," they say, when I
am so alive I ache with it
so much I do not look alive
but chase that cock-teaser till
my balls so ache with her
that I fall groaning into speech
and write the one word RAPE
on subway lavatory walls
while she, receptive but to me,
dances and sings around me:
"Yes and no and maybe so
and everywhere all over." Oh
my nonsense: she's the truth;
I cry the sentence of the Fool:
"I don't know what to do!"
Her left eye winks Yes,
her right eye stares No,
and her smile smiles smiles
while I write copy for
her disappearance on the air!
as "Miss Unknowable, 1964."

CONSPIRACY OF TWO AGAINST THE WORLD

If I were out of love
and sequence I would turn
the end of love—its death—
knifelike against myself
to cut off my distinction and
rejoin the Commons, maimed.
But love is here!, so by
that contact with the one
oh may I contact all
self-alienated aliens
in Atom City and apply
to join the one big union.
Workers of this world, unite!

Once, when I liked a German girl,
hating the Krauts but loving the tongue
in a loving mouth, I'd make her say
"Apple!" that crucial word, and feel
like Tenzing and Hillary on Everest,
   breathless and drinking hot lemonade
      to a victory dried out of nationalism,
         class, and caste, and drunken back
            to the Garden's original purity on the heights!
Later I lapsed into hate and lost
the taste of her mouth in division.

on horseback, and
the saber's drawn,
lunar acuity
cut out a slice
of sunlight in mid-air.
He whirled it once
around his head, a halo, and
discharged it at a foe.
Charge forever, hero! Rear,
horse! The saber points
toward death, by means
of which he changed
into a statue in the square.
To you the glory, brother,
and to us the girls.

NARCISSUS II

I used to beg for roses in the garden of love
and got them. The couples laughed and paid.
Not any more. Now the ladies do not smile.
Their gentlemen draw swords and order me away.
I went to look in Narcissus' public pool,
weeping and asking why. I had a beard! I saw,
and heard the answer: "Figure it out for yourself:
you must have grown up blind to be a fool.
Isn't there something you should want to do
or die?" "Oh remarkable absence of joy, what is it?"
A sword broke surface toward me, point first.
Then her hand around the hilt appeared,
and then herself, smiling. "Here it is," she said,
"from point to hilt and hand: take it either way."

POEM

It is no wonder that new lovers run
rice gantlets to Niagara Falls
or to some other elephant wonder:
once weightless love finds bodying
in the archaic landscapes of the flesh
it needs proportion in its flow
and goes to public waters. There
it falls asleep unoverwhelmed
while fall sounds shake the panes
of Sweetheart Cottages & Darling Hotel,
and wakes up ordinarily disposed to say:
"I gained ten pounds!", "We never got
to see the Falls!", or, "All is well."

Oh put the elephant in chains.
His must is dangerous.
Three tons of love in pain
run trumpeting over us.

Flowering balls!,
roses are coming on
in solar systems oh
galactic rose bush. By
tomorrow, given rain,
roses will be out for bees.
It's yours and mine, wild
rose, to open to for love,
its stingers and its rain,
but it is Its always.

The birth of Seventh Avenue
from Varick Street at night
is out of surf, all moonshine
as it breaks along the curb,
coming, flooding, and falling away.
In it, matter's savagery
extrudes a civic fault, a man
wading in moonlight blocks
away, hunchbacked in the shape
of things before my birth,
beyond my death, and now,
panicked by night alive.
I fear the animal embrace
of Venus' negative half-
creature of the universe,
whose wildness, let in out of love,
must be the genius of this place.

On coming up on deck Palm Sunday morning, oh
we saw the seas the dancy little tourist ship
climbed up and down all night in cabin dreams.
They came along in ridges an horizon wide!
and ran away astern to the Americas we left,
to break on headlands and be called "the surf."
After services below, the pilgrims to the east
carried their processed palm fronds up on deck
and some of them went overboard from children's hands.
So, Christ: there were the palm leaves on the water
as the first fruits of the ocean's promised land.
They promise pilgrims resurrection out at sea,
though sea-sick fasters in their bunks below
cry out for harbor, order, and stability.
This is the place for it! The sky is high
with it, the water deep, the air its union: spray!
We all walk the water just below the decks
too, helplessly dancing to the world's variety
like your Jerusalem, Byzantium, and Rome.

Now that autumn is over and all
that increase has been reaped or wasted,
a dead tree and the dead vines on it
scrape together in the wind as strings and bows.
This is so it can be said of listeners:
"They heard playing," before the snow
falls thicker and thicker until the air
is all snow. Then, when we dig out
of it into the upper air, those sounds
will have been buried from the air
and we will hear the silence above the tree.
This is so it can be said of listeners:
"They heard silence," not: "They never heard
a thing about the music underneath them."

Two main diseases, con-
sciousness and dreams, demand
it, a division of the whole.
Then   Then
the   around   the
flesh   the   mind
weeps   speech-   weeps
to   less   to
itself   center: itself
alone   alone
That by this simple split
the subtler be rejoined: then
flesh sings in its throat,
the speechless center spreads
its wings, and Nothing says
an eagle! taking sustenance
from animals of the ground.

The broken glass on the stairs
shines in the electric light.
Whoever dropped the beer
was anti-social or too drunk
to sweep it up himself.
So the beauty goes, ground
under heel but shining, it
and the deposit lost. But
by the janitor's broom
it is still sharp enough
for dogs' feet, babies' hands,
and eyes pierced by its lights,
that he should curse the fool
and I should try to praise
the pieces of harmony.

I have found my figures,
love, and I am theirs
to do with as we will.
Oh they got sucked into the void
spaces of an infant skull
because a storm blew up in there
around a cataclysm: birth.
They fought as winged lions
until they fouled the waste
with carrion and living jaws
and almost died: their ghosts
still roar around on the air
above the desert floor
but leave objective room,
lamb, for your material:
love. Oh it is here
that I propose to build
it, the cathedral "Abattoir":
it is a concrete fold, in plan,
with columned lions to mark
it, set in a desert storm.
Please be its visitor.

DATE DUE

GAYLORD			PRINTED IN U.S.A.